Title - Solitary Dancer
ISBN 13 - 978-1-955144-12-4
Composer - Andrew T Hanna
Graphic Design, Layout, & Artwork - Andrew T Hanna
Copyright - 2023
Genre - jazz-fusion/jazz-rock

Solitary Dancer composed in the spring of 1999 after watching a senior showcase dance performance at UARTS. The dance routine began slow and accelerated to a breath taking speed. The music from this dance was of a steady drone that became rhythmic during the second half of the performance. These aspects are reflected in Solitary Dancer. This composition combined time changes, ostinatos, and two opened solo sections. This composition was composed during a time when I realized the many limitations of both jazz and academic jazz. Much of academic jazz music taught doesn't allow for exploration of the aforementioned musical aspects.

Until next time.

Andrew Hanna

Score

Solitary Dancer

Andrew Hanna

Solo Section

Interlude

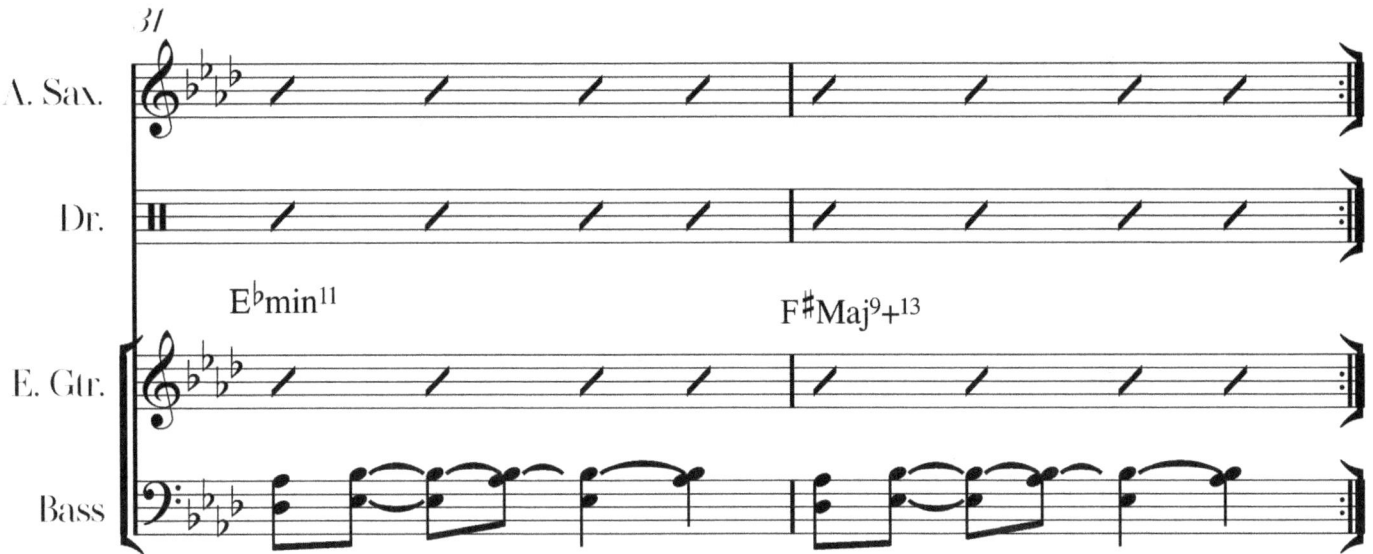

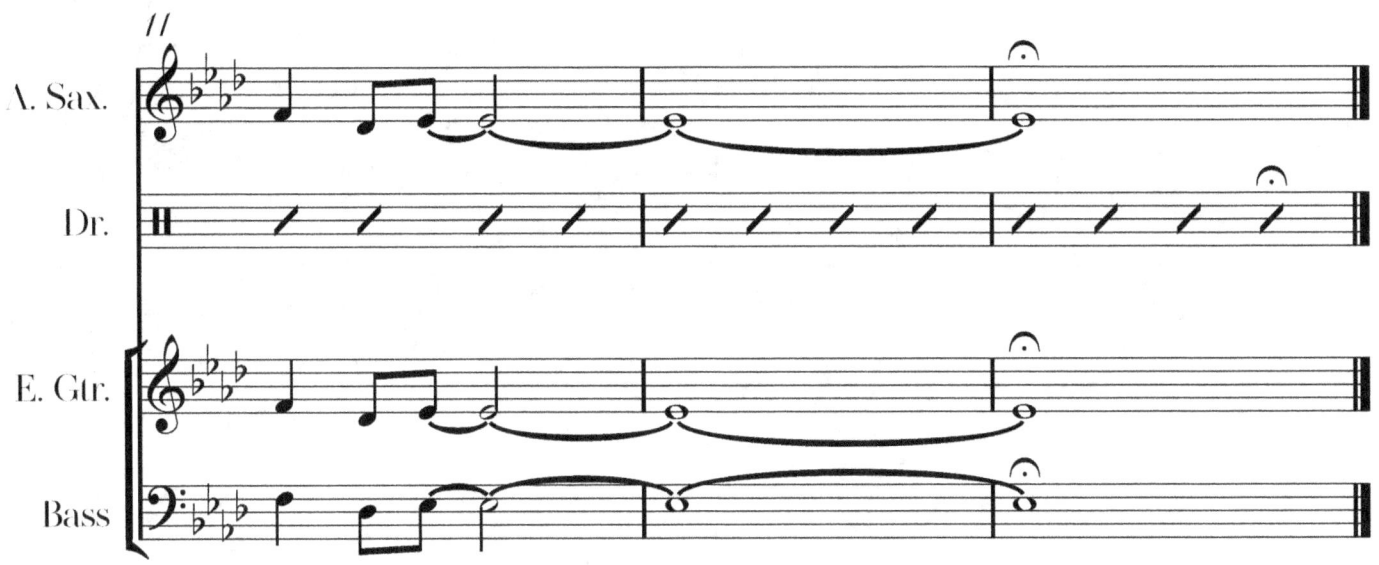

Alto Saxophone

Solitary Dancer

Alto Sax

Andrew Hanna

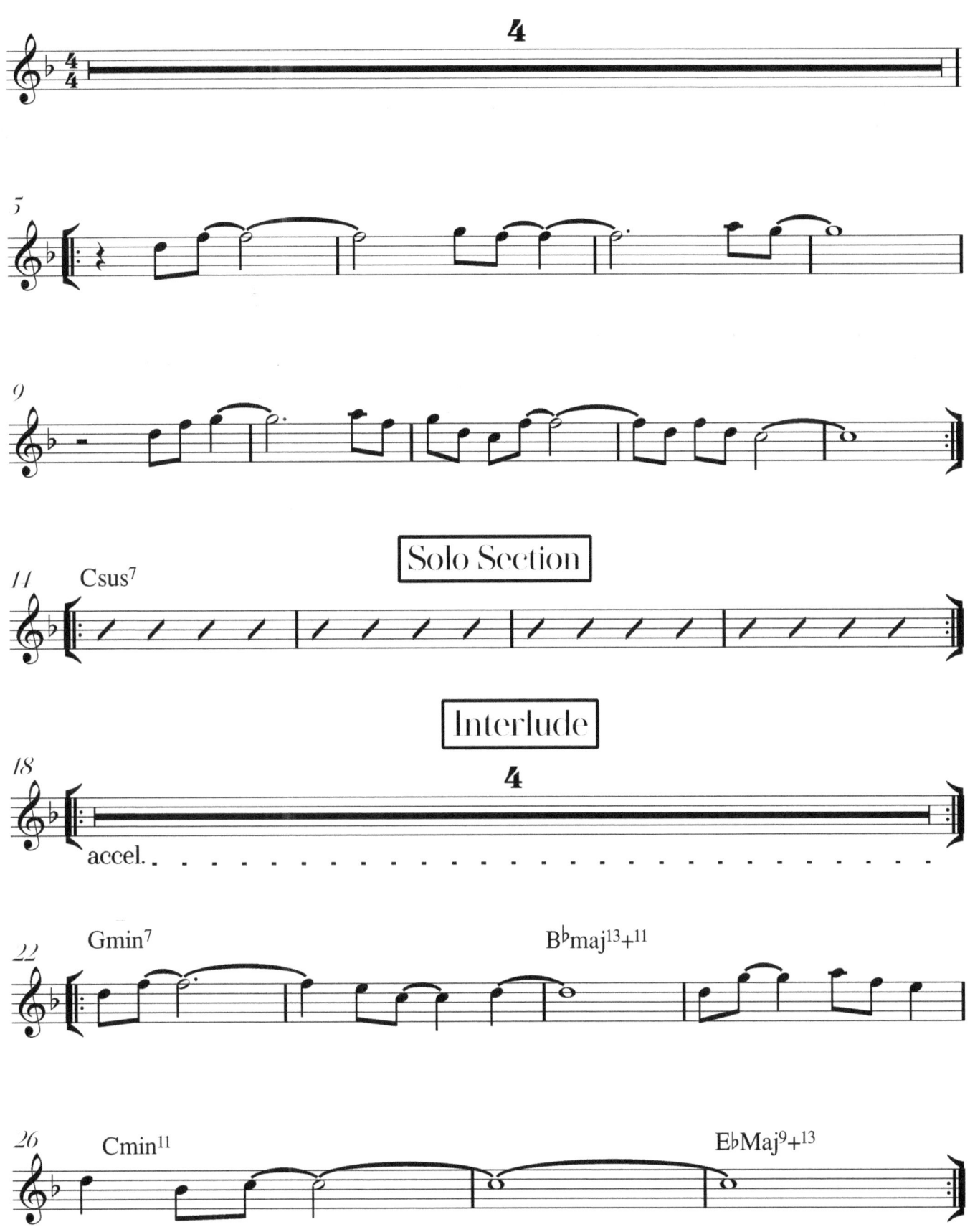

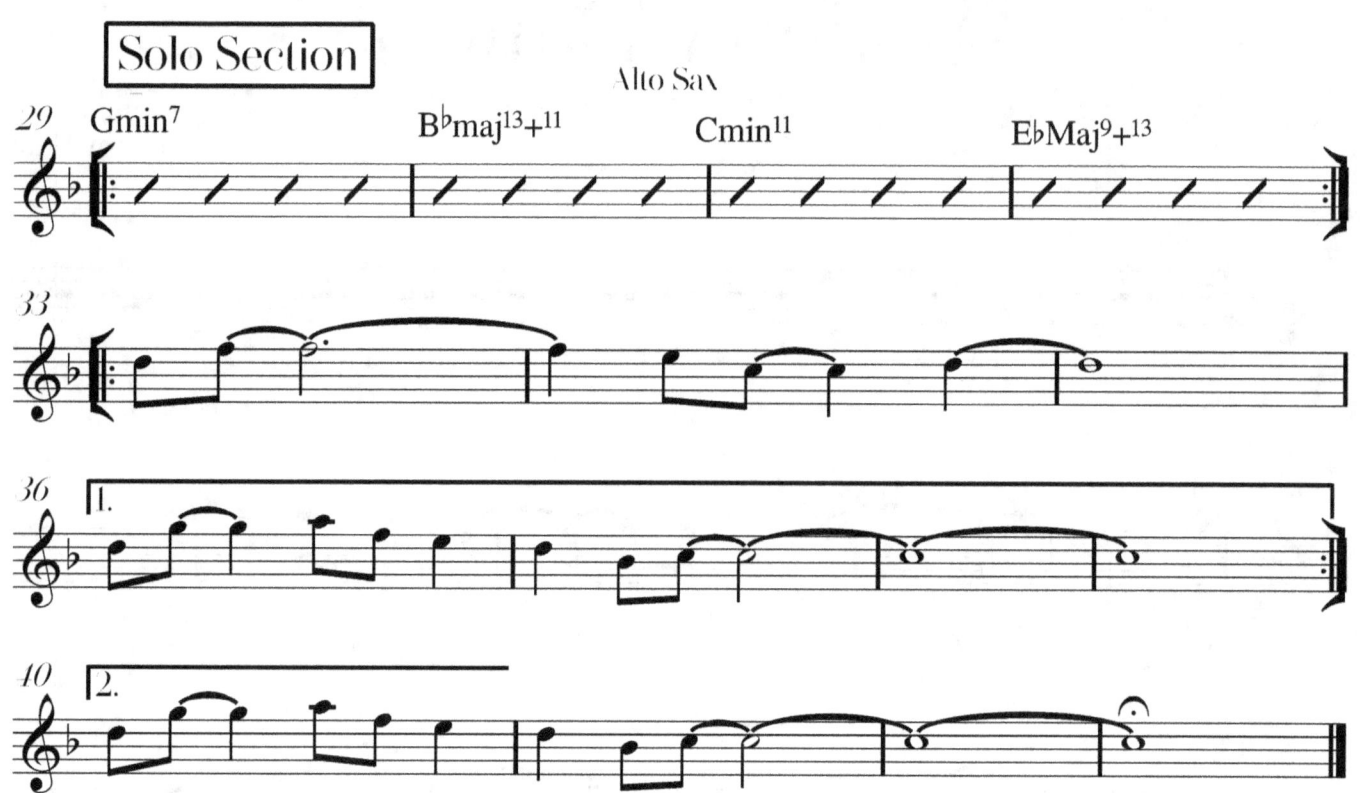

Solo Section

Alto Sax

29 Gmin^7 B♭maj^{13}+^{11} Cmin^{11} E♭Maj^9+^{13}

33

36   1.

10   2.

ElecTric GuiTar

Solitary Dancer

Electric Guitar

Andrew Hanna

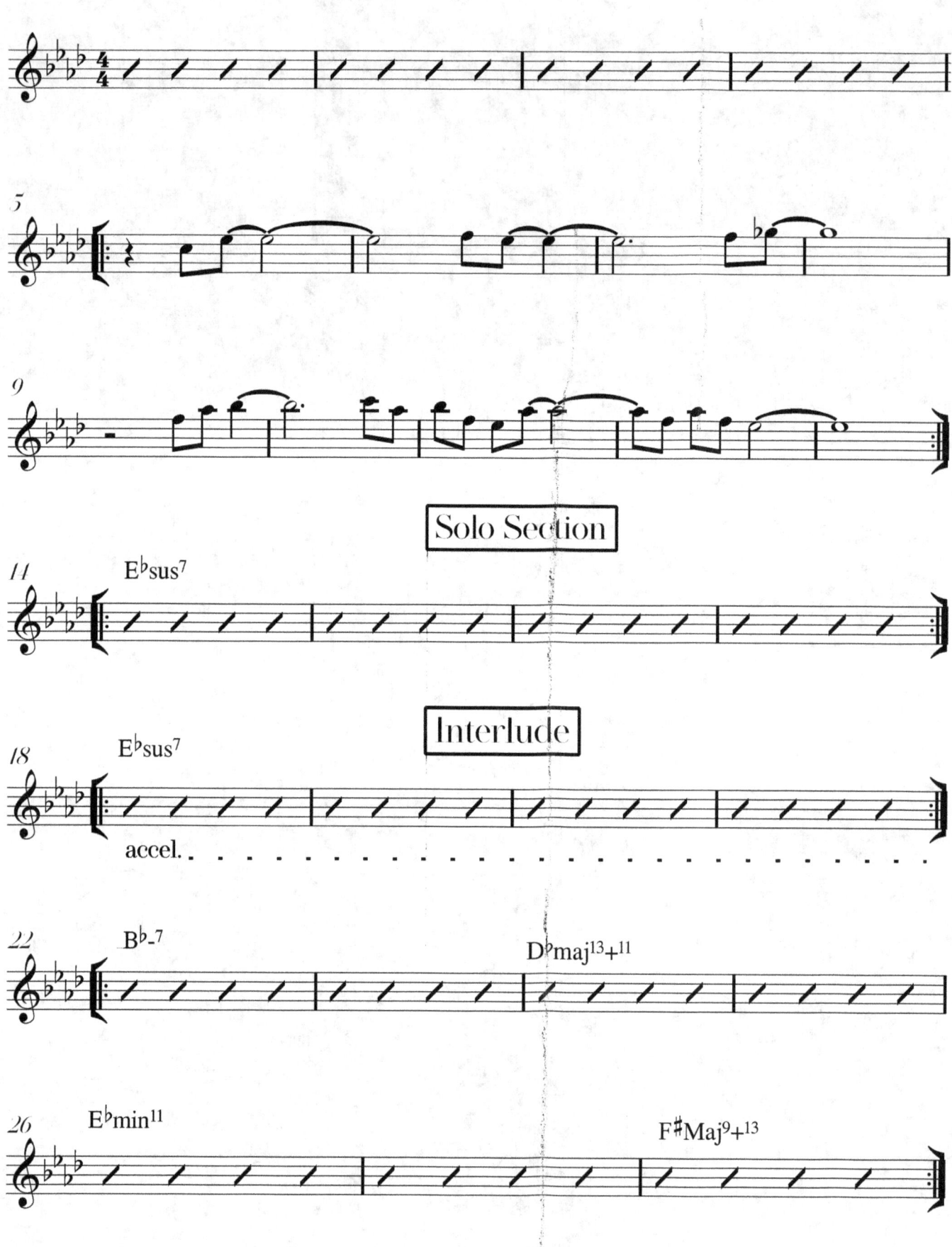

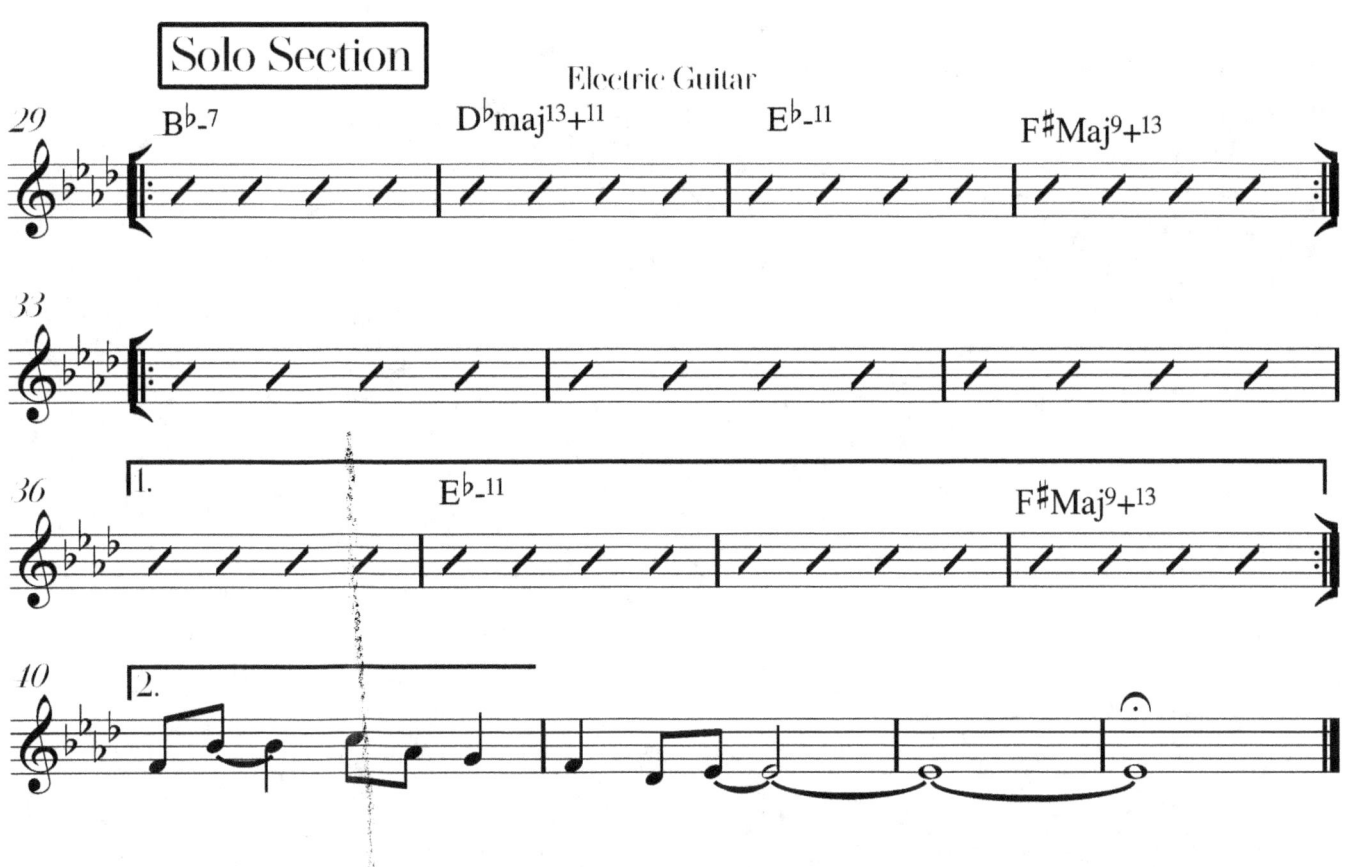

BAss
GuitAr

Solitary Dancer

Bass Guitar

Andrew Hanna

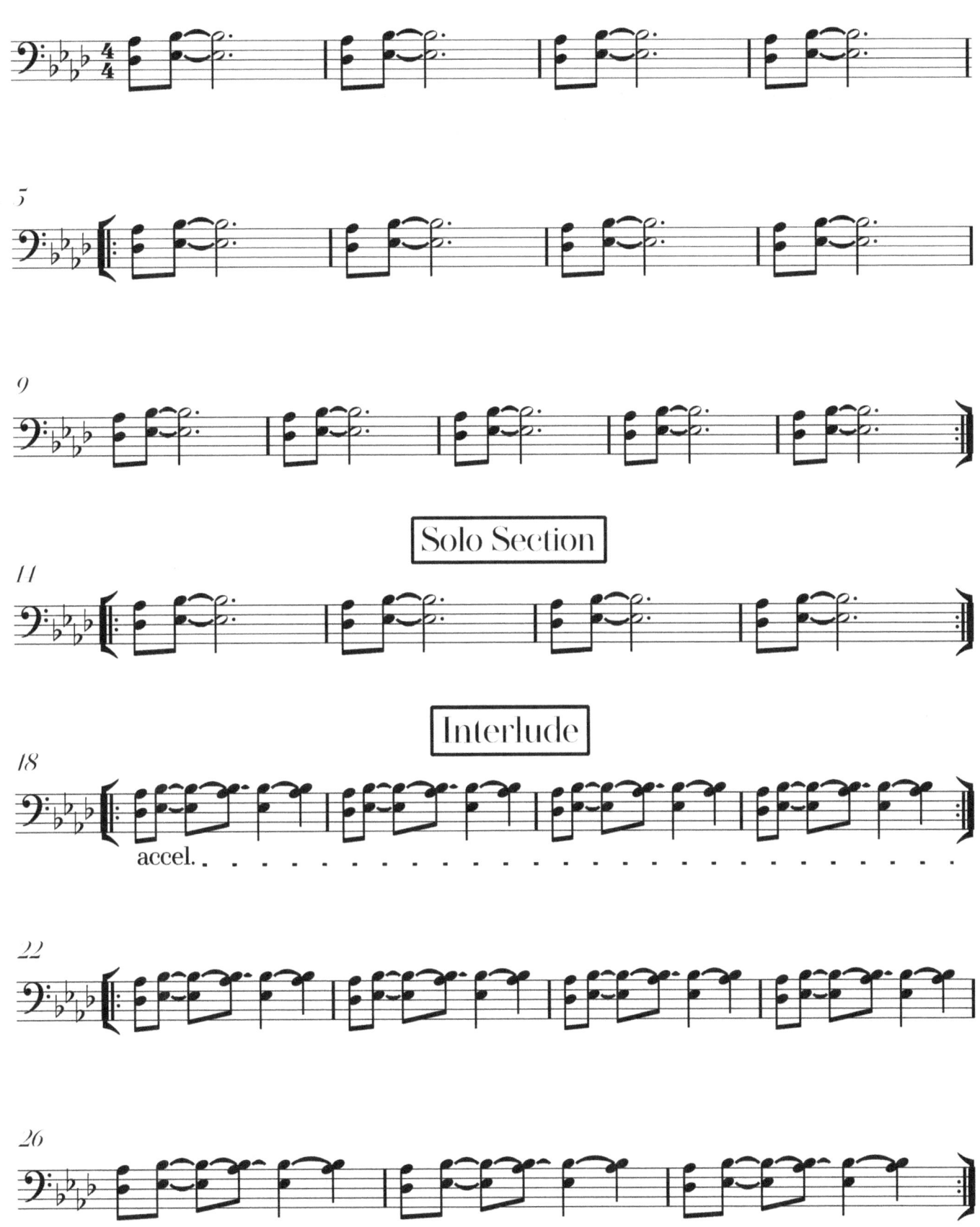

Solo Section

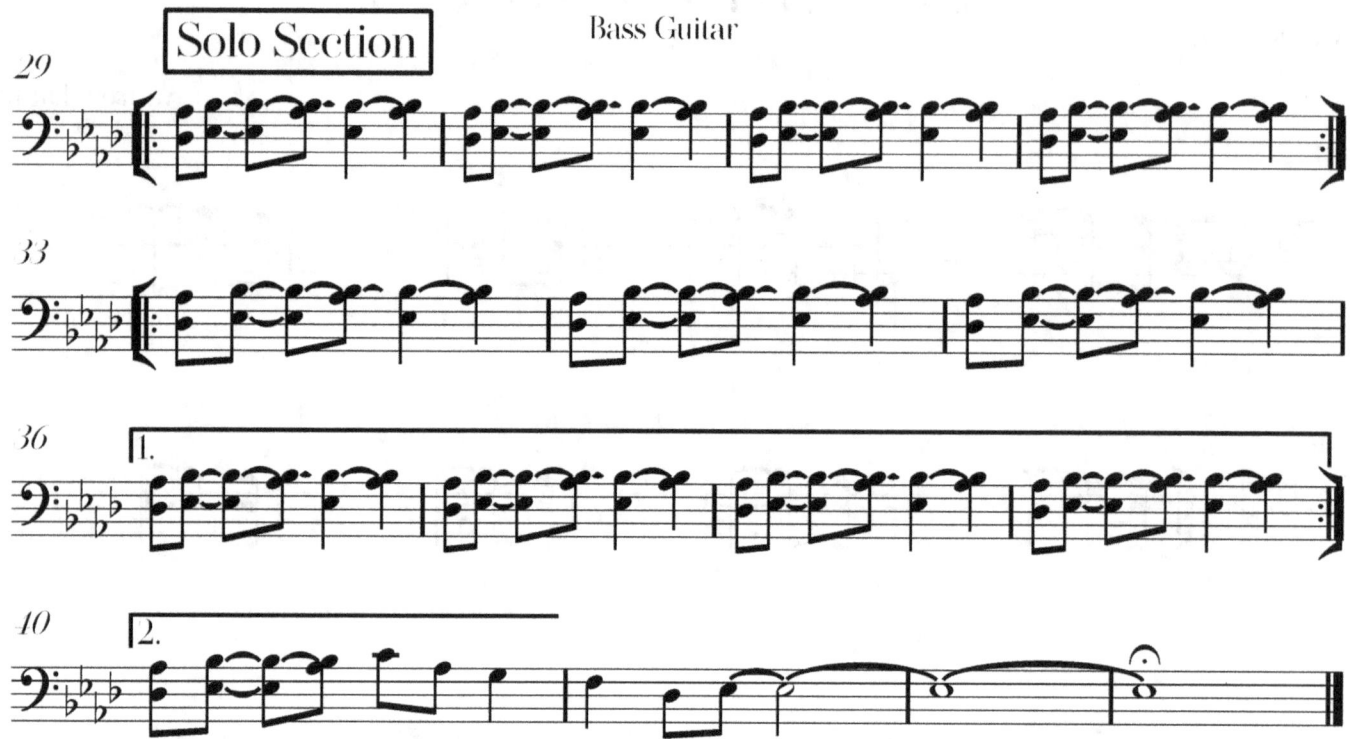

DrumSet

Solitary Dancer

Drum Set

Andrew Hanna

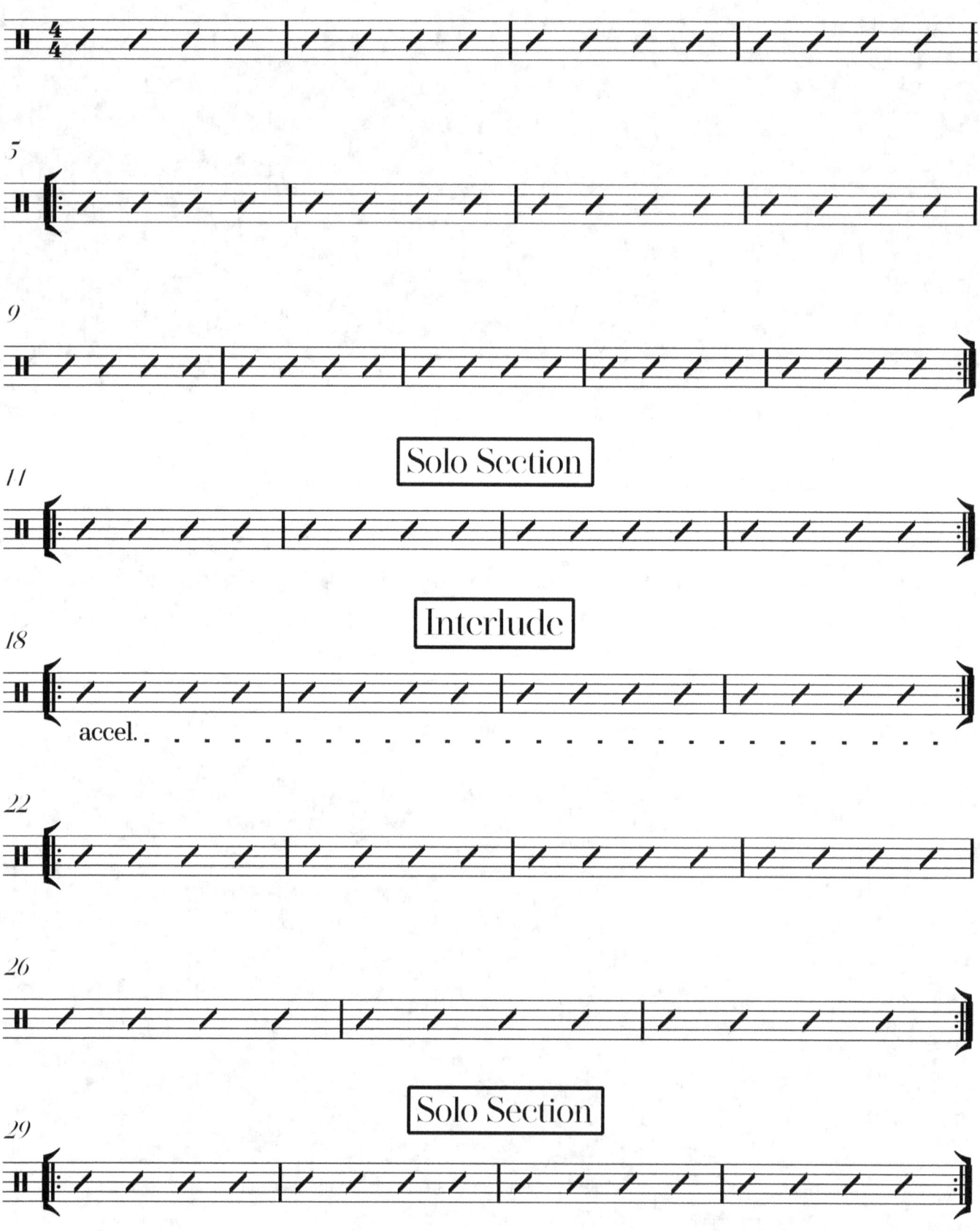

Solo Section

Interlude

accel.

Solo Section

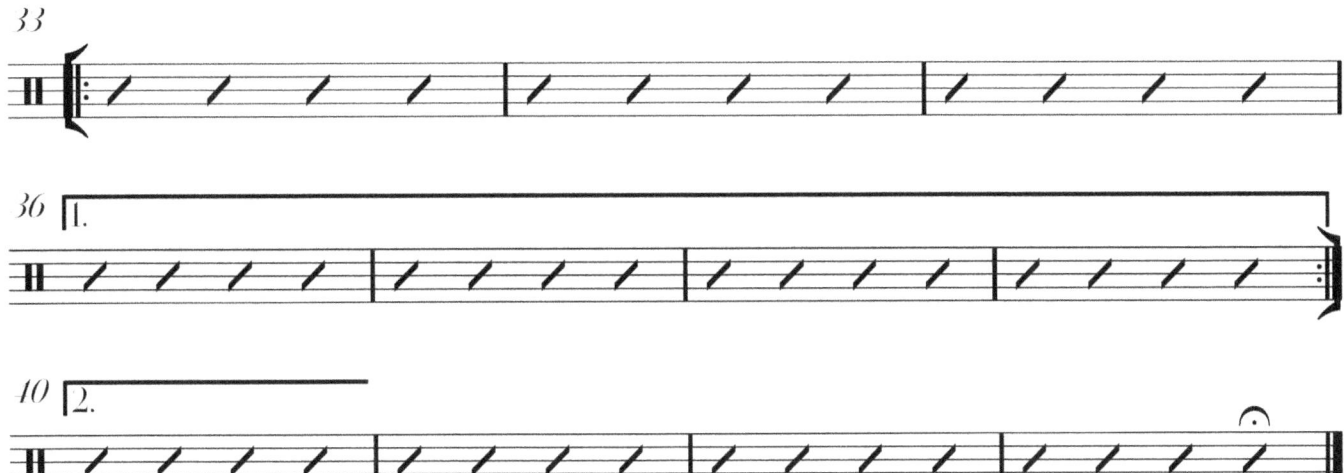

Other Compositions by Andrew Hanna

In the Beginning (from Prophecies of War)

ISBN13 - 978-1-955144-04-9

Genre – Jazz Fusion/Jazz Rock/Prog Rock

Instruments - Alto Sax, Keys, Drums, Bass, Guitar

The Yard Cat Song

ISBN13 - 978-1-955144-02-5

Genre - Straight Ahead Jazz Quartet

Instruments - Alto Sax, Piano, Drums, Bass

A Change of Heart

ISBN13 - 978-1-955144-08-7

Genre - Jazz Fusion/Jazz Rock

Instruments - Alto Sax, Drums, Bass

In Walked Dolphy

ISBN13 - 978-1-955144-00-1

Genre - Straight Ahead Jazz Quartet

Instruments - Alto Sax, Piano, Drums, Bass

Earth, Wind, Water, Fire

ISBN13- 978-1-955144-06-3

Genre - Jazz Fusion/Jazz Rock

Instruments - Soprano Sax, Alto Sax, Tenor Sax, Piano, Drums, Bass, Guitar

Profit-C (from Prophecies of War)

ISBN13- 978-1-955144-10-0

Genre - Jazz Fusion/Jazz Rock/Prog Rock

Instruments - Alto Sax, Keys, Drums, Bass, Guitar